IT'S TIME TO EAT WHITE CHEDDAR MAC AND CHEESE

It's Time to Eat WHITE CHEDDAR MAC AND CHEESE

Walter the Educator

Silent King Books
A WhichHead Entertainment Imprint

Copyright © 2024 by Walter the Educator

All rights reserved. No part of this book may be reproduced in any manner whatsoever without written per- mission except in the case of brief quotations embodied in critical articles and reviews.

First Printing, 2024

Disclaimer

This book is a literary work; the story is not about specific persons, locations, situations, and/or circumstances unless mentioned in a historical context. Any resemblance to real persons, locations, situations, and/or circumstances is coincidental. This book is for entertainment and informational purposes only. The author and publisher offer this information without warranties expressed or implied. No matter the grounds, neither the author nor the publisher will be accountable for any losses, injuries, or other damages caused by the reader's use of this book. The use of this book acknowledges an understanding and acceptance of this disclaimer.

It's Time to Eat WHITE CHEDDAR MAC AND CHEESE is a collectible early learning book by Walter the Educator suitable for all ages belonging to Walter the Educator's Time to Eat Book Series. Collect more books at WaltertheEducator.com

USE THE EXTRA SPACE TO TAKE NOTES AND DOCUMENT YOUR MEMORIES

WHITE CHEDDAR MAC AND CHEESE

It's time to eat, oh what a treat,

It's Time to Eat
White Cheddar Mac and Cheese

A bowl of warmth, so cheesy and sweet.

White cheddar melts, a creamy delight,

Dinner is here, let's take a big bite!

The noodles wiggle, a happy little dance,

They twirl on my fork, I give them a chance.

Soft and cozy, they slip and slide,

White cheddar magic fills me with pride.

Steam rises up, the smell so yummy,

I can't wait to fill my hungry tummy!

A sprinkle of love, a dash of cheer,

White cheddar mac is the meal I hold dear.

Grab your spoon or your fork, take a seat,

This cheesy delight can't be beat!

One bite, two bites, three and four,

White cheddar mac makes me ask for more.

It's Time to Eat
White Cheddar Mac and Cheese

The creamy sauce wraps each noodle tight,

Oh, this dish is pure delight.

It's a hug in a bowl, so warm and snug,

Each cheesy bite feels like a big hug.

Mmm, so tasty, the flavor's just right,

White cheddar mac brings smiles tonight.

With every spoonful, my heart feels glad,

No better meal when I'm feeling sad.

Look at the bowl, it's almost done,

Eating white cheddar mac is so much fun.

But there's still a little, just one more bite,

Oh, what a dinner, my favorite tonight!

Now my tummy is full, my plate is clean,

The cheesiest meal I've ever seen.

White cheddar mac, you're my best friend,

I can't wait to eat you again!

So let's give thanks for this cheesy dish,

Warm and creamy, my mealtime wish.

Time to clean up, but I'm still grinning,

It's Time to Eat
White Cheddar Mac and Cheese

White cheddar mac makes every meal winning!

With a happy heart and a cheerful grin,

I'm ready to start this night's adventures again.

But I'll dream of noodles and cheesy bliss,

White cheddar mac, you're my mealtime kiss!

ABOUT THE CREATOR

Walter the Educator is one of the pseudonyms for Walter Anderson. Formally educated in Chemistry, Business, and Education, he is an educator, an author, a diverse entrepreneur, and he is the son of a disabled war veteran. "Walter the Educator" shares his time between educating and creating. He holds interests and owns several creative projects that entertain, enlighten, enhance, and educate, hoping to inspire and motivate you. Follow, find new works, and stay up to date with Walter the Educator™

at WaltertheEducator.com

www.ingramcontent.com/pod-product-compliance
Lightning Source LLC
LaVergne TN
LVHW052016060526
838201LV00059B/4053